COLLECTIONS

A Harcourt Reading / Language Arts Program

*Special times
and
special friends
go together.*

COLLECTIONS

A Harcourt Reading / Language Arts Program

SPECIAL TIMES

SENIOR AUTHORS

Roger C. Farr • Dorothy S. Strickland

AUTHORS

Richard F. Abrahamson • Alma Flor Ada • Bernice E. Cullinan • Margaret McKeown • Nancy Roser
Patricia Smith • Judy Wallis • Junko Yokota • Hallie Kay Yopp

SENIOR CONSULTANT

Asa G. Hilliard III

CONSULTANTS

Karen S. Kupiter • David A. Monti • Angelina Olivares

Harcourt

Orlando   Boston   Dallas   Chicago   San Diego

Visit *The Learning Site!*
www.harcourtschool.com

ISBN 0-15-319080-9

1 2 3 4 5 6 7 8 9 10   048   2003 2002 2001 2000

Dear Reader,

Get ready to share some **Special Times** with some special friends. Read about what happens when animals and other things can talk! Learn about being a friend and about trying new things.

There are lots of adventures to share when you read. Turn the pages and let the fun begin!

Sincerely,

The Authors

The Authors

Contents

theme

I Think I Can!

Reader's Choice

Shoe Town

by Susan Stevens Crummel and Janet Stevens

A little mouse is joined by many friends as they make a town of shoes!

Award-Winning Author/Illustrator

FROM THE LIBRARY

Big Brown Bear

by David McPhail

Big Bear wants to paint a
playhouse for Little Bear,
but he has some trouble.

Award-Winning Author/Illustrator
FROM THE LIBRARY

Mr. Gumpy's Outing

by John Burningham

Mr. Gumpy takes
a boat ride with all
of his friends!

ALA Notable Book

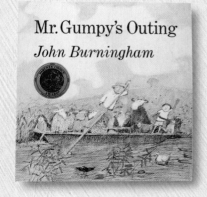

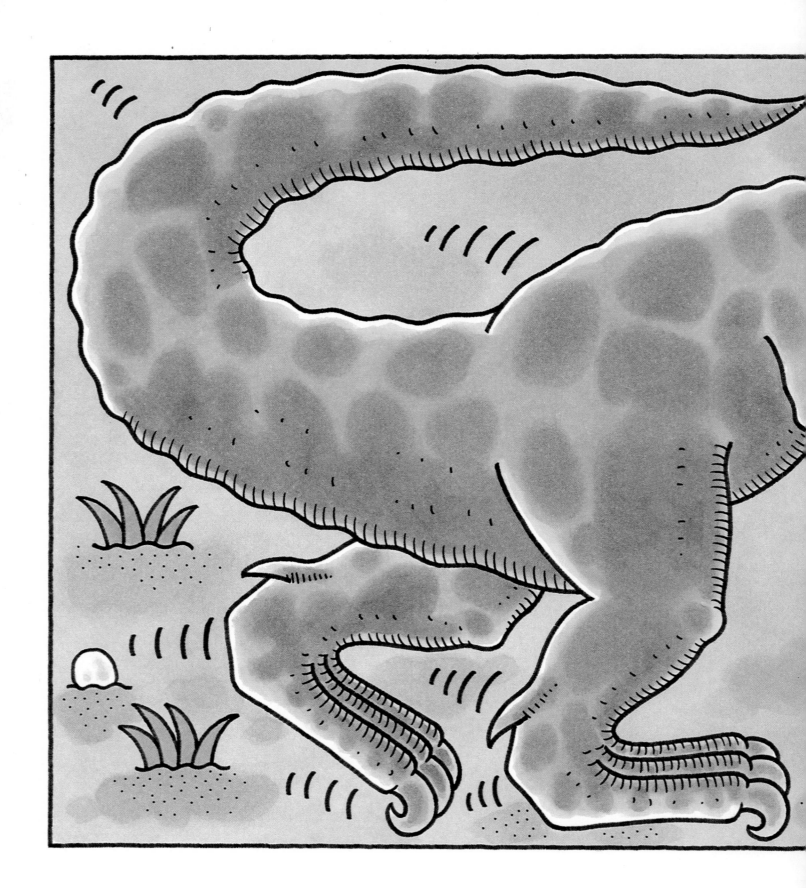

Catch Me If You Can!

by Bernard Most

Award-Winning
Author/Illustrator

He was the biggest dinosaur of them all. The other dinosaurs were afraid of him.

When the biggest dinosaur went by,
the other dinosaurs quickly hid.

They were afraid of his
great big tail.

They were afraid of his
great big claws.

They were afraid of his
great big feet.

But most of all, they were afraid
of his great big teeth.

One little dinosaur wasn't afraid.
She didn't run. She didn't hide.

"Catch me if you can!" she called
to the biggest dinosaur.

"I'm not afraid of your
great big tail."

"Catch me if you can!"

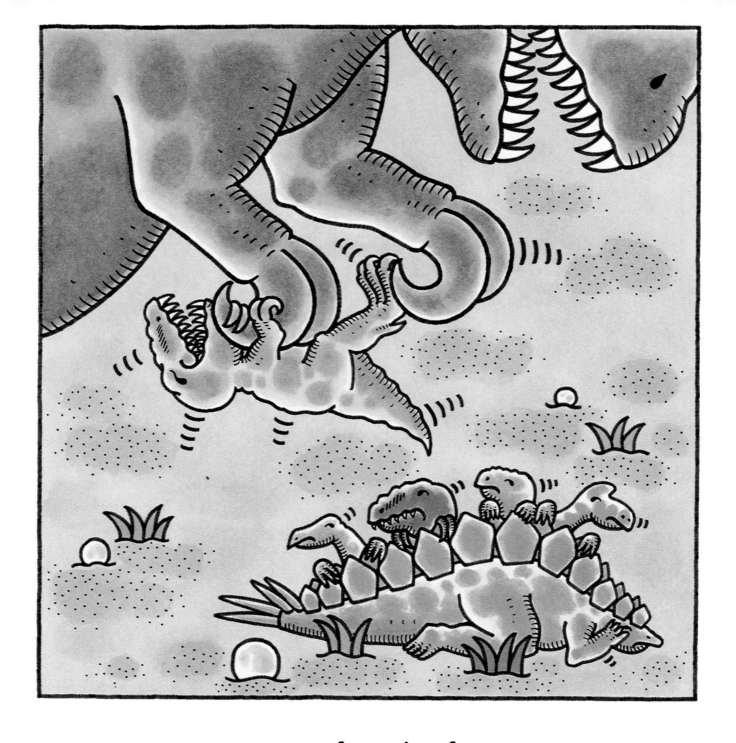

"I'm not afraid of your
great big claws."

"Catch me if you can!"

"I'm not afraid of your
great big feet."

"Catch me if you can!"

"And most of all, I'm not afraid
of your great big teeth."

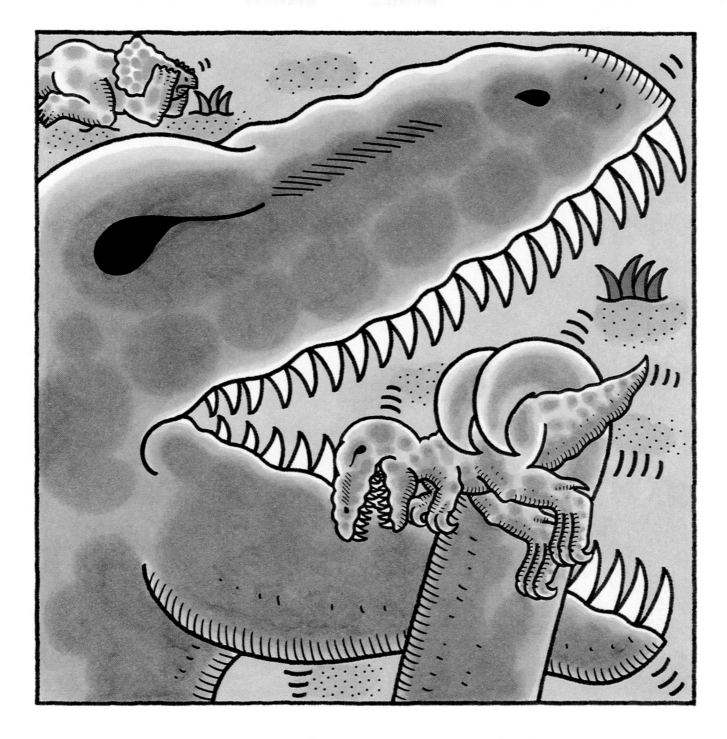

"I can catch you!" said the
biggest dinosaur. And he
grabbed the little dinosaur.

But she only got a big hug.
"I love you very much, Grandpa!"
said the little dinosaur.

"And I love you, too!" said the
biggest dinosaur of them all.

Meet the Author/Illustrator
Bernard Most

Bernard Most knew he wanted to be an artist even before he went to kindergarten. Later, he went to art school and became an artist. He saw some books by Leo Lionni and liked them so much that he started to write his own books for children.

Bernard Most works hard on his books. He sent out one book 42 times before it was published! He didn't give up. He knows how important it is to believe in yourself and to keep trying.

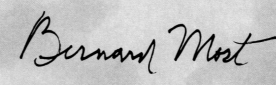

Visit *The Learning Site!*
www.harcourtschool.com

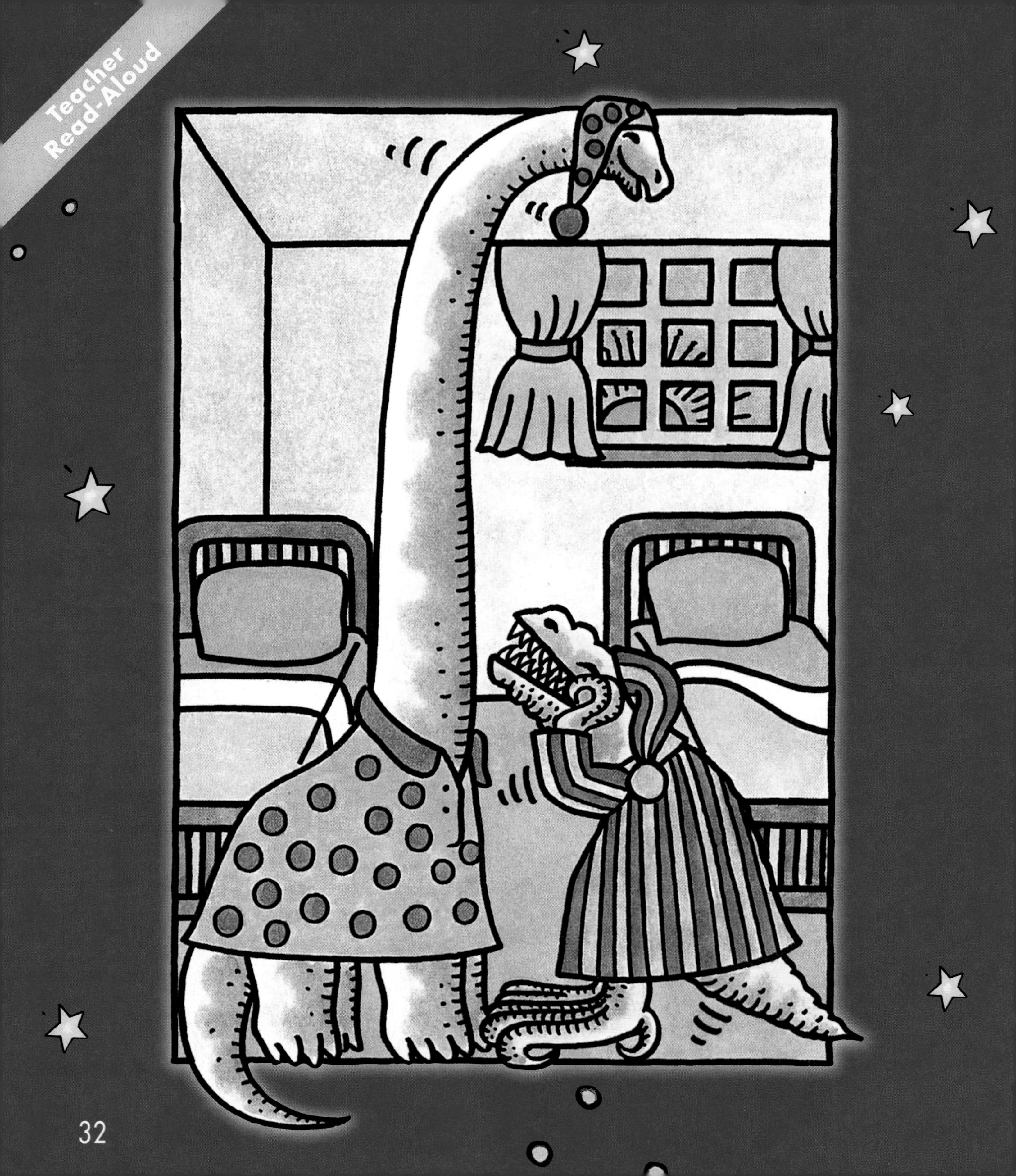
Teacher
Read-Aloud

DINOSAUR
Words of Wisdom

by Bernard Most

Go to bed late,
Stay very small.
Go to bed early,
Grow very tall.

DINOSAUR TAG

Play a dinosaur game with a big group of children.

1 Line up. Put your hands 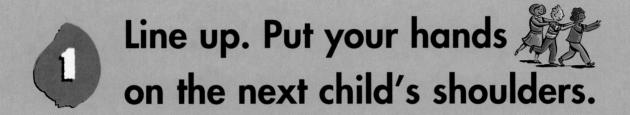 on the next child's shoulders.

2 The first child is the head. The last child is the tail.

3 The head tries to catch the tail.

If the head catches the tail, play again!
If the line breaks, the head goes to the tail. Then play again.

When the TV Broke

by Harriet Ziefert

pictures by Mavis Smith

Award-Winning
Author

Jeffrey watched television
every day of the week.

Jeffrey watched on Monday . . .

on Tuesday . . .

on Wednesday . . .

on Thursday . . .

on Friday . . .

and on Saturday.

On Sunday
right in the middle
of a gorilla movie—

the TV made a loud "buzz!"
The picture faded and . . .

the screen went black.

Jeffrey's mom turned
all the dials.
But nothing happened.

On Monday Jeffrey's dad
put the TV into the car.

47

Jeffrey sat on the sofa.
Now he had nothing to do.

49

On Tuesday Jeffrey asked,
"Is the TV fixed yet?"

"Not yet," Jeffrey's mom said.
"Maybe tomorrow."

On Wednesday Jeffrey said,
"It's tomorrow.
Is the TV fixed yet?"

"Not yet," she said.
"Maybe tomorrow."

On Thursday Jeffrey said,
"It's tomorrow.
Is the TV fixed yet?"

"Not yet," Mom said.
"Maybe tomorrow."

"What are you doing?"
asked Jeffrey's sister.
"Nothing much," he said.

"Will you read to me?"
she asked.
"Okay," said Jeffrey.

57

Then it was Friday.

Jeffrey found some boxes.

He found paint . . .
scissors . . . crayons . . .
and glue, too.

59

"What are you doing?"
asked Jeffrey's sister.

"Nothing much," he said.

"What are you doing now?"
asked Jeffrey's sister.

"Nothing much,"
he said.

63

On Saturday Dad called,
"I'm home! Come and watch TV.
It's all fixed!"

64

65

"Not now, Dad," said Jeffrey.
"I'm busy. Maybe tomorrow."

Meet the Author

Harriet Ziefert

Like her character Jeffrey, Harriet Ziefert likes to make things. She buys old eggbeaters, nutcrackers, and other kitchen tools and uses them to make sculptures.

One sculpture she made looks like a bug. Another looks like a mouse. "It's fun to dig through piles of junk at a flea market to find old objects," says Harriet Ziefert. "But making a new treasure out of the old things is even more fun!"

Harriet M. Ziefert

Visit *The Learning Site!*
www.harcourtschool.com

RESPONSE ACTIVITY

Make a Calendar

What do you do on different days of the week? Make a calendar that shows something you do each day for a week.

Monday

I played socc

Wednesday

I went out for pizza with my family.

Monday	Tuesday	Wednesday	Thursday	Friday	Saturday	Sunday
I played soccer.	I made a puppet.	I went out for pizza with my family.	I went for a walk with my parents.	I read a book.	I had a soccer game.	I played with my friends.

1 Fold a sheet of paper in half (the long way).

2 Cut along the fold. Tape the pieces together to make a long strip.

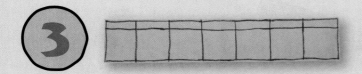

3 Write the days of the week at the top of your calendar.

4 Draw and write about something you do each day for a week.

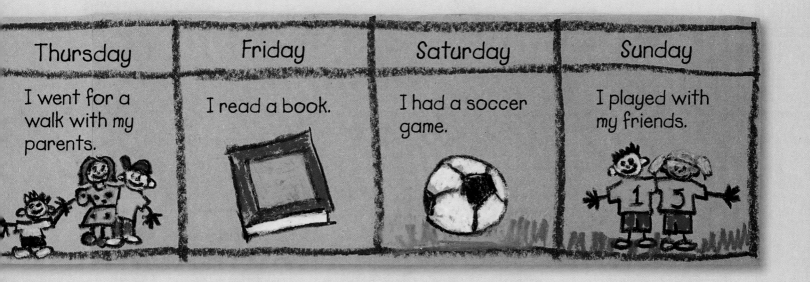

Thursday	Friday	Saturday	Sunday
I went for a walk with my parents.	I read a book.	I had a soccer game.	I played with my friends.

Share your calendar with a classmate.

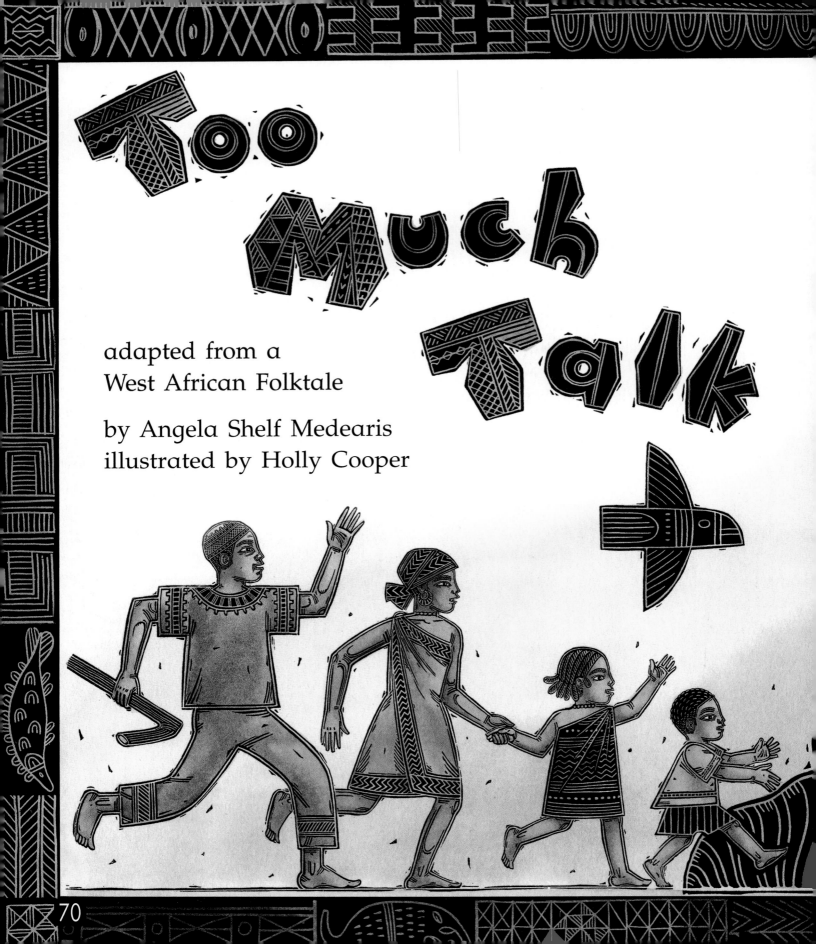

Too Much Talk

adapted from a
West African Folktale

by Angela Shelf Medearis
illustrated by Holly Cooper

Characters

Storyteller

Farmer

Farmer's Wife

Older Child

Younger Child

Yam

Dog

Fisherman

Fish

Weaver

Cloth

Swimmer

Lake

Chief

Chair

Today's story starts with a farmer and his family sitting down to lunch.

 Mother, I'm hungry!

 I'm hungry, too. I want some yams.

 We don't have any yams.

 But we always have yams.

 I could eat yams every day! Yum, yum!

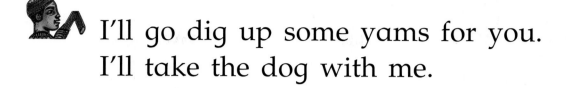 I'll go dig up some yams for you.
I'll take the dog with me.

The farmer walks out with the dog.
Soon the farmer starts to dig.

77

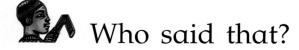 You planted me and left me here.
Now here you come to dig me up!

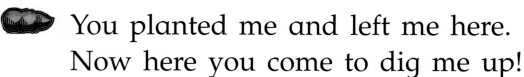 Who said that?

It wasn't me! The yam must have said it.

Aiee!

The farmer runs away as fast as he can. He passes a man who is fishing.

 Why are you running in the heat of the day? Stop and sit with me.

 I can't! I must see the chief.

Why do you want to see the chief?

Well, first my yam talked. Then my dog talked.

81

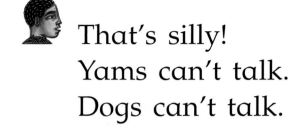 That's silly!
Yams can't talk.
Dogs can't talk.

 Oh yes, they can!

 Aiee!

 They run away as fast as they can. They pass a weaver.

83

Why are you running in the heat of the day? Stop and sit with me.

We can't! We must see the chief.

84

 Why do you want to see the chief?

 Well, first my yam talked. Then my dog talked.

85

Then my fish talked! Talk, talk, talk!

 Too much talk!

 That's silly!
Yams and dogs can't talk.
Fish can't talk.

 Oh yes, they can!

 Aiee!

 They run away as fast as they can. They pass a woman swimming in the lake.

 Why are you running in the heat of the day? Stop and swim with me.

 We can't! We must see the chief.

Why do you want to see the chief?

 Well, first my yam talked. Then my dog talked.

 Then my fish talked!

89

Then my cloth talked! Talk, talk, talk!

 Too much talk!

That's silly!
Yams can't talk.
Dogs can't talk.
Fish can't talk.
Cloth can't talk.

Oh yes, they can!

91

 Aiee!

 They all run away as fast as they can.
They come to the chief's house.

Chief! Chief! Help us!
Help us!

The chief comes out and sits in his chair.

93

 What's all the fuss about? Why are you running in the heat of the day?

 Well, first my yam and my dog talked.

 Then my fish talked!

 Then my cloth talked!

 Then the lake talked! Talk, talk, talk!

 Too much talk!

That is very silly!
Yams and dogs don't talk.
Fish and cloth don't talk.
Lakes don't talk.

 Oh yes, they do!

96

 Aiee!

They all run away as fast as they can. Will they get away from all this talk?

THE END

ANGELA SHELF MEDEARIS

Angela Shelf Medearis is a storyteller as well as a writer. When she tells the story "Too Much Talk!" to children, she has them act it out with her. Angela Shelf Medearis believes that acting is one of the best ways to express ourselves. She hopes you have fun acting out "Too Much Talk!"

Angela Shelf Medearis

Meet the Illustrator
HOLLY COOPER

Holly Cooper is an illustrator, but she also loves clothes and sewing. Before she began to paint the pictures for "Too Much Talk," she looked at pictures and pieces of cloth from West Africa. This helped her paint clothes that the fisherman, weaver, chief and other characters might really have worn.

Holly Cooper

Visit *The Learning Site!*
www.harcourtschool.com

99

Sahara Desert

MAURITANIA

Sénégal R.

SENEGAL

GAMBIA

Niger R.

NIGER

MALI

CHAD

GUINEA
BISSAU

GUINEA

BURKINA

Sokoto R.

NIGERIA

AFRICA

SIERRA
LEONE

IVORY
COAST

LIBERIA

GHANA

TOGO

BENIN

CAMEROON

EQUATORIAL
GUINEA

ATLANTIC
OCEAN

West Africa and Its Food

written by Alison Brownlie

Millet and Corn

Millet and corn are both grain crops, like rice. Grain crops are among the main foods for most people in West Africa.

Fish

Fish and seafood are an important source of protein for people who live near the coast or a river.

Yams and Cassava

Yams and cassava are the other main foods in West Africa. They are both root vegetables, which means that they grow underground.

Peanuts

Peanuts, which are also called groundnuts, are really a type of bean. They are a main food crop in the dry north.

Cattle, Sheep, and Goats

These animals are kept mainly for their milk. Farmers in the north move their cattle around in herds and sell them for meat.

Fruit

Fruits such as mangoes, coconuts, pineapples, and bananas grow on plantations, as well as in the wild.

In the play, the farmer's dog talked. What would we hear if we could understand what animals say? Make a page for a class book about what the animals are saying.

- Choose an animal.

- Think about what it might say.

- Draw and write about what your animal says.

Share your page with classmates.
Put the pages together to make a
class book.

Making Friends, Keeping Friends

WRITTEN BY ELIZABETH DAVIS   PHOTOGRAPHS BY LILLIAN GEE

Making Friends, Keeping Friends

What is a friend?

What can you do with friends?

108

Let's make up a game of our own.

A friend is someone you want to be with—

and who wants to be with you.

Do you want
to come over?

Yes! I'll be
right there!

A friend is someone who helps you—

and someone you help, too.

Sometimes math
is like a puzzle.

You're right! Will you help
me add these up?

A friend is someone you can talk to—
and who wants to talk to you.

I like bugs the best.

Not me! I like tigers.

Sometimes friends make things.

It's fun to be a team.

I'll get the bagels.

Good! I'll be as quick as
I can with these eggs.

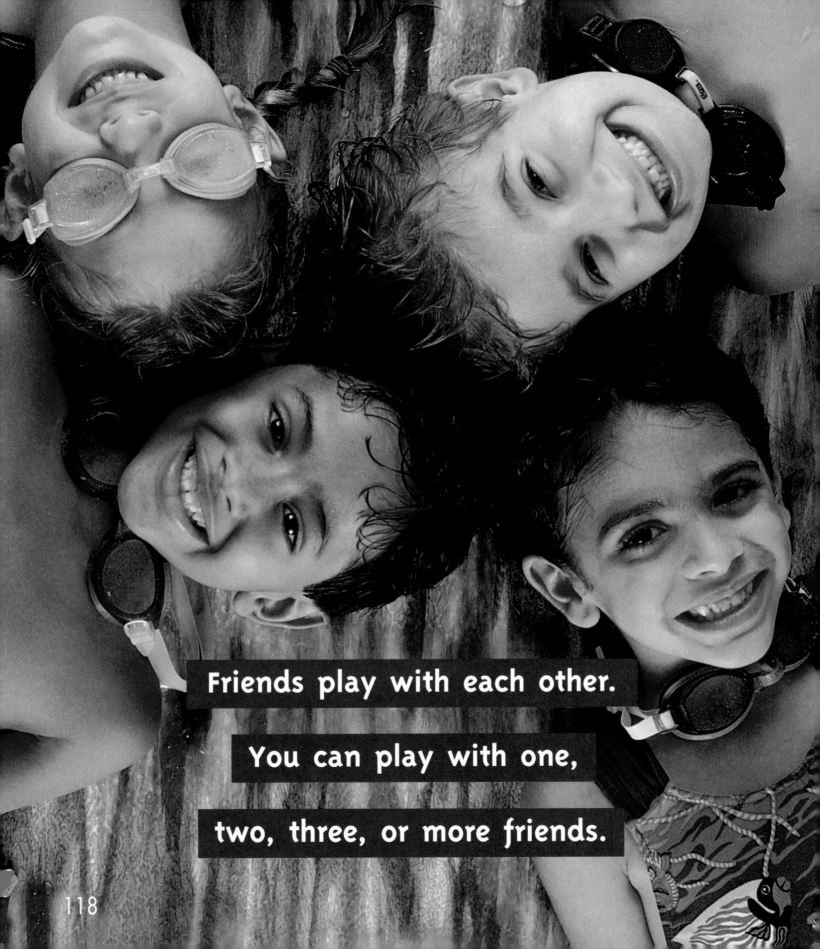

Friends play with each other.
You can play with one,
two, three, or more friends.

Let's go swimming!

I can't wait to jump in!

Sometimes friends get mad at each other.

But they talk things over.

Thanks for playing ball with me.

It was fun! Next time
I'll choose the game.

Friends like to do things for each other.

They answer each other's questions.

What is this word?

It says "birthday."

It does? I didn't know that!

A friend is someone you can count on—
and who can count on you!

Meet the Photographer

Lillian Gee

Lillian Gee loves taking pictures of children. She says, "Children are fun to work with because they always surprise you."

After hearing the story "Making Friends, Keeping Friends," Lillian Gee had one thing to add about friendship. "Always tell the truth to your friends and to yourself."

Lillian Gee

 **Visit *The Learning Site!*** www.harcourtschool.com

Your Own Camera

Lillian Gee is a photographer.
You can be a photographer, too!

1 Fold a piece of paper in half. Tape the sides.

2 Make it look like a real camera.

3 Draw some pictures. Put them inside your camera.

4 "Develop" your film and share your pictures with classmates.

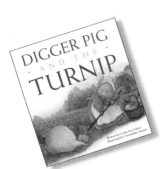

DIGGER PIG
✦ AND THE ✦
TURNIP

WRITTEN BY CARON LEE COHEN
ILLUSTRATED BY CHRISTOPHER DENISE

One day Digger Pig dug up a big
turnip. "I can use this to make a
good turnip pie," she said.

Chirper Chick, Quacker Duck, and Bow-Wow Dog sat around in their corner of the barn. "Let's make a turnip pie," said Digger Pig. "Who will help me cut the turnip?"

"Not I," said Chirper Chick.
"Not I," said Quacker Duck.
"Not I," said Bow-Wow Dog.

"All right then. I will cut the
turnip myself."

And she did.

Then Digger Pig asked, "Who will help me mash the turnip?"

"Not I," said Chirper Chick.
"Not I," said Quacker Duck.
"Not I," said Bow-Wow Dog.

134

"All right then. I will mash
the turnip myself."

And she did.

Next, Digger Pig asked,
"Who will help me make
the pie?"

"Not I," said Chirper Chick.
"Not I," said Quacker Duck.
"Not I," said Bow-Wow Dog.

"All right then. I will make
the pie myself!"

And she did.
She called her piglets to supper.

"Can we have some pie?" the others asked.

"No!" grunted Digger Pig. "You didn't help. My piglets and I will eat it all."

And they did!

Meet the Author
CARON LEE COHEN

Caron Lee Cohen thinks of herself as a cook, like Digger Pig. She says that writing a story is a lot like preparing food. You have to mix together the right ingredients and then taste the dish to know if it is just right!

Caron Lee Cohen

Meet the Illustrator
CHRISTOPHER DENISE

Christopher Denise

Christopher Denise likes drawing animals. Before he starts to draw, he looks at pictures of real animals to get ideas. He says, "I know children will like a story even more if the animals are really special."

Visit *The Learning Site!*
www.harcourtschool.com

141

Act It

Have a
Digger Pig
puppet
show.

1 Draw Digger Pig
and her friends.
Cut them out.

2 Tape on craft
sticks to make
puppets.

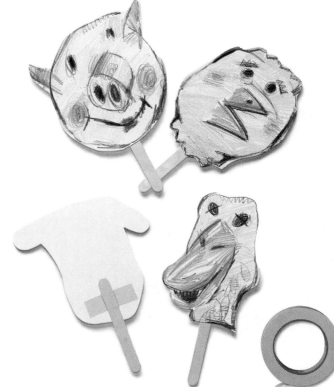

Out!

3 Think of new stories for Digger Pig and her friends.

4 Have a puppet show.

REX AND LILLY

Playtime

Award-Winning
Author
and
Illustrator

by Laurie Krasny Brown

illustrated by Marc Brown

"Time for dance class, Rex," said Mom.
"Let's go now."

"Not me! Not now!" said Rex.
"I don't want to dance."

"Just try!" said Mom.

"How shall we warm up?" the dance teacher, Ms. Tiptoe, asked the class.

149

"Push-ups," said Rose.

"Jumping jacks," said Jack.

"Hot cocoa," said Rex.

The class warmed up.
They did push-ups.

They did jumping jacks.

Rex warmed up, too.

"Time to dance now!" said Ms. Tiptoe.
"I will show you how.

Boys, you dance *forward step, back step, slide, slide, slide.*
Girls, you dance *back step, forward step, slide, slide, slide.*"

"Now you try! Ready?" said Ms. Tiptoe.
The boys did the steps.
The girls did the steps.

Rex did the steps, too.

"Good!" said Ms. Tiptoe. "Girls, please pick a boy to dance with."
"Not me! Not now!" said Rex.

Then Rose asked Rex, "Will you
dance with me?"
"Me? Now?" asked Rex.
"Yes!" said Rose.

"Now for the music," said Ms. Tiptoe.
"Let's dance!"

Rose danced *back step, forward step,
slide, slide, slide.*
Rex danced *forward step, back step,
slide, slide, slide.*

They danced on and on.

"See you next time, boys and girls!"
said Ms. Tiptoe.
"Let's go, Rex," said Mom.
"Not me! Not now!" said Rex.
"I did try, and I do want to dance!"

Meet the Author

Laurie Krasny Brown

Dear Readers,

Many of my story ideas come from being around children like you. I like to use my imagination, too. Don't you feel good when you try something new and find out it's fun? I do! This story is about one of those times.

Your friend,

Laurie Krasny Brown

 Visit *The Learning Site!* www.harcourtschool.com

Meet the Illustrator

Marc Brown

Dear Readers,

I remember when my mother made me take dance lessons every Tuesday night. I felt the same way that Rex did in the story. Now my wife, Laurie, and I take dance classes together. It's a lot more fun!

Your friend,

Marc Brown

RESPONSE ACTIVITY

DINOSAUR DANCE

Rex learns to dance. Work with a group to make up a dinosaur dance that Rex would like to do.

Dance Steps:

- **forward step**
- **back step**
- **slide**
- **stomp**
- **sway**
- **wiggle**
- **twirl**
- **bend**

1 Pretend to be a dinosaur. **2** Make up your dance steps.

3 Add music. ♪ Use props, if you want:

balloons streamers scarves ankle bells.

4 Practice your dance. **5** Now do your dance for an audience.

Acknowledgments

For permission to reprint copyrighted material, grateful acknowledgment is made to the following sources:

Harcourt, Inc.: Cover illustration from *Where to Look for a Dinosaur* by Bernard Most. Copyright ©1993 by Bernard Most. Cover illustration from *How Big Were the Dinosaurs?* by Bernard Most. Copyright ©1994 by Bernard Most. Cover illustration from *The Littlest Dinosaurs* by Bernard Most. Copyright ©1989 by Bernard Most.

HarperCollins Publishers: Cover illustration by S. D. Schindler from *How Many Fish?* by Caron Lee Cohen. Illustration copyright ©1998 by S. D. Schindler. From *Four and Twenty Dinosaurs* (Retitled: "Dinosaur Words of Wisdom") by Bernard Most. Copyright ©1990 by Bernard Most. Cover illustration by Simms Taback from *Who Said Moo?* by Harriet Ziefert. Illustration copyright ©1996 by Simms Taback.

Holiday House, Inc.: Cover illustration by John Ward from *Poppa's New Pants* by Angela Shelf Medearis. Illustration copyright ©1995 by John Ward.

Henry Holt and Company, Inc.: Cover illustration from *Mr. Gumpy's Outing* by John Burningham. Copyright ©1970 by John Burningham.

Just Us Books: Cover illustration by Anna Rich from *Annie's Gifts* by Angela Shelf Medearis. Illustration copyright 1994 by Anna Rich.

Little, Brown and Company (Inc.): "Let's Dance" from *Rex and Lilly: Playtime* by Laurie Krasny Brown, illustrated by Marc Brown. Copyright ©1995 by Laurene Krasny Brown and Marc Brown. Cover illustration from *Arthur's Pet Business* by Marc Brown. Copyright ©1990 by Marc Brown. Cover illustration from *Dinosaurs Travel* by Laurie Krasny Brown and Marc Brown. Copyright ©1988 by Laurie Krasny Brown and Marc Brown. Cover illustration from *D. W. the Picky Eater* by Marc Brown. Copyright ©1995 by Marc Brown. Cover illustration from *Dinosaurs Alive and Well* by Laurie Krasny Brown and Marc Brown. Copyright ©1990 by Laurie Krasny Brown and Marc Brown. Cover illustration from *D. W. Thinks Big* by Marc Brown. Copyright ©1993 by Marc Brown.

Walter Lorraine Books, an imprint of Houghton Mifflin Company: Cover illustration by Donald Saaf from *Elemenopeo* by Harriet Ziefert. Illustration copyright ©1998 by Donald Saaf.

Scholastic Inc.: Cover illustration by Christopher Denise from *Little Raccoon Catches a Cold* by Susan Canizares. Illustration copyright ©1998 by Christopher Denise. A Scholastic SidebySide Book.

State House Press: Cover illustration by Charles Shaw from *Picking Peas for a Penny* by Angela Shelf Medearis. Copyright ©1990 by State House Press.

Steck-Vaughn Company: From *Food and Festivals: West Africa* by Alison Brownlie. Text copyright ©1999 by Steck-Vaughn Company.

Viking Penguin, a division of Penguin Putnam Inc.: *When the TV Broke* by Harriet Ziefert, illustrated by Mavis Smith. Text copyright ©1989 by Harriet Ziefert; illustrations copyright ©1989 by Mavis Smith.

Photo Credits

Key: (T)=top, (B)=bottom, (C)=center, (L)=left, (R)=right
Page 31, Walt Chrynwski / Black Star; 34, 35, Campos Photography; 67, Rick Falco / Black Star; 68, 69, Ken Karp / Harcourt; 98, 99, Bob Daemmrich Photography; 101(t), Betty Press / Panos Pictures; 101 (b), Wayland Picture Library; 102(t), Tim Durham / Eye Ubiquitous; 102(b), Jeremy Hartley / Panos Pictures; 103(t), Liba Taylor / Panos Pictures; 103(b), Ron Giling / Panos Pictures; 104, 105, Ken Karp / Harcourt; 106-123, Lillian Gee / Picture It, Corp.; 124, Jade Albert / FPG; 125, Lillian Gee / Picture It, Corp.; 126, 127, Campos Photography; 141(t), Walt Chyrnwski / Black Star 141(b) Rick Friedman / Black Star; 142, 143, Campos Photography; 164, 165, Rick Friedman / Black Star; 167, Campos Photography.

Illustration Credits

Will Terry, Cover Art; Gary Taxali, 4-9; Bernard Most, 10-32; Mavis Smith, 36-67; Holly Cooper 70-99; Connie McLennan, 100; Christopher Denise, 128-141; George Kreif, 142-143; Marc Brown, 144-165